Mel Bay's
Celtic Guitar
ENCYCLOPEDIA

Fingerstyle Guitar Edition

by Glenn Weiser

This book is for Patti

1 2 3 4 5 6 7 8 9 0

Visit us on the Web at www.melbay.com — E-mail us at email@melbay.com

CONTENTS

INTRODUCTION

Celtic music is as beautiful as it is vast and varied. With their red-blooded pipe marches, tender harp airs, vivacious dance tunes, and lovely songs, few parts of the world can claim such musical wealth as Ireland and Scotland. This music seems endless — French-Canadian fiddler Jean Carignan, for example, is said to have known 7,000 tunes.

But of course none of this music was composed for the guitar, and the instrument itself wasn't even played much in Ireland until the 1940's. With the folk boom of the sixties, fingerpickers started to work out arrangements of fiddle tunes. And even though a number of Celtic guitar books have since been published, they represent only a tiny fraction of the traditional repertory.

This book contains over one hundred Celtic tunes for solo guitar. It is part of a collection of almost three hundred arrangements I have done over the last twenty years. Two volumes — *Folk Songs for Solo Guitar* and *Celtic Harp Music of Carolan and Others for Solo Guitar* — have already appeared; now I can offer guitarists even more.

The book is divided into four sections. The first part consists of airs, marches and waltzes. Famous tunes like *Londonderry Air, The Parting Glass,* and *All Through the Night* are included, as well as those lesser known but equally worthy. Here you'll find marches where the guitar mimics the bagpipes, plaintive laments for fallen heroes, tunes that are sheer whimsy, and love songs of great beauty and passion.

In the second section there are reels, jigs, and hornpipes. For almost two hundred years beginning around 1675, step dancing was the national pastime in Ireland. During this period the fiddle was the dominant instrument, and thousands of dance tunes were composed by anonymous musicians. Traveling dancing masters made their livings teaching new steps wherever they went, and it was not unheard of for a whole village to drop its labors to greet a teacher of the art when he showed up in town. Most of the tunes in this section date from this period.

In 1792 it was realized that the Irish harp, which had been the nation's most loved instrument since ancient times, was fast dying out. To collect and preserve what was still left of this music, a gathering of harpers was organized in Belfast to compete for cash prizes. Ten harpers came to the festival, and a young church organist, Edward Bunting, was hired to write down the tunes. Although his work was flawed by his failure to notate the bass parts of the pieces, Bunting did preserve many of the oldest Irish airs. He arranged the material for piano (adding a few questionable accidentals along the way), and in the same year authored the first volume of *The Ancient Music of Ireland*. He later toured Ireland, collecting more music from harpers, singers, and other musicians, and eventually produced two further volumes. Tunes from the Bunting Collection — harp pieces, songs, and a jig — make up the third part.

Turlough O' Carolan (1670-1738) was the last of the great Irish harper-composers. Blinded by smallpox at eighteen, he had been given three years of harp lessons and then sent out on the road as an itinerant musician. He soon learned he had a creative gift and would compose tunes for the wealthy patrons who provided him with hospitality in exchange for music. In the mansions of the aristocracy he came to admire Italian Baroque music and attempted to incorporate elements of it into his often remarkable pieces. His music was later collected and his biography written by the Irish scholar Donal O'Sullivan. Over twenty of Carolan's tunes (214 have survived) conclude the book.

These arrangements are all in standard tuning or dropped D, which makes them viable for both nylon and steel string guitars. They have also been worked out in the original keys whenever possible so that they may be performed with other instruments used in Celtic music. In writing the bass lines and inner voices I have followed the rules of four-part voice leading because I like the way the tunes sound with simple diatonic harmony. Indeed, I often think of arranging traditional music as being similar to jewelry making — the tune itself is the gem, and the harmonization and the fingering are the setting. To be displayed, the stone needs the setting, and the setting in turn must do justice to the stone.

I'd like to thank Bill Bay of Mel Bay Publications for bringing out this book, and also John Roberts for engraving the music.

Any correspondence regarding this book may be addressed to me at P.O. Box 2551, Albany, NY, 12220. Enjoy the tunes.

Glenn Weiser

Airs, Marches, and Waltzes

All Through The Night

*Musicologists consider this famous Welsh lullaby one of the most beautiful of all folk melodies.
I learned it from the singing of Bill Morgan, an old friend and traveling companion.
The variations at the end are my own.*

Traditional Welsh
Arranged by Glenn Weiser

2ND VARIATION

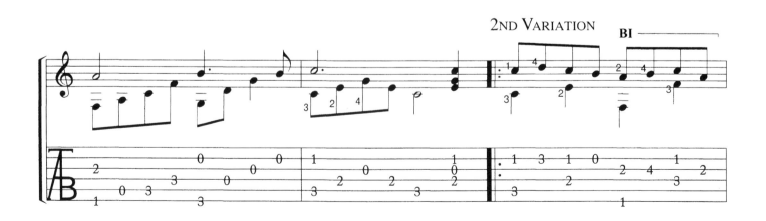

The Atholl Highlanders

At Blair Castle in Scotland, the Duke of Atholl maintains the last private standing army in Europe, the Atholl Highlanders. This arrangement attempts to mimic the Highland pipes by having the right hand thumb and index finger pinch two bass strings to make a drone while the middle and ring fingers play the tune in the treble. There are four parts.

Traditional Scottish
Arranged by Glenn Weiser

8

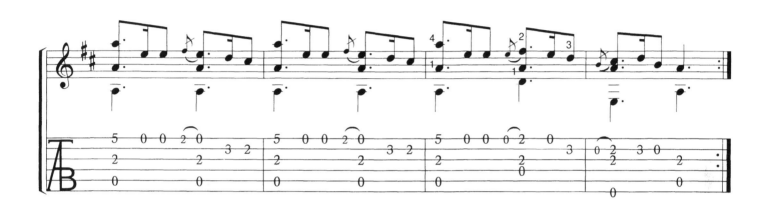

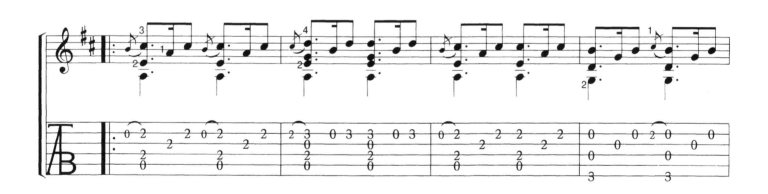

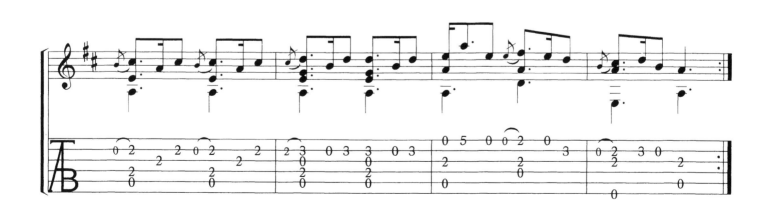

The Banks of Inverness

I learned this Scottish march from upstate New York fiddler Mark Bagdon.
The town of Inverness is located at the head of Loch Ness in the Highlands.

Traditional Scottish
Arranged by Glenn Weiser

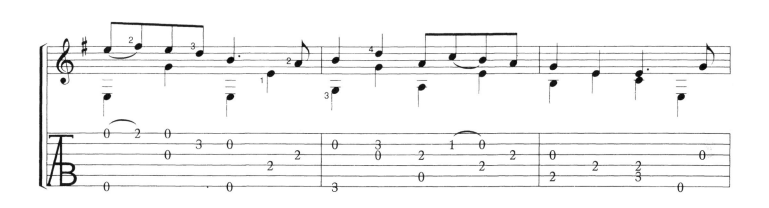

The Battle of Waterloo

This Highland pipe march commemorates Napoleon's final defeat of 1815.
It has been worked out in the same style as "The Atholl Highlanders."

Scottish Pipe March
Arranged by Glenn Weiser

Believe Me If All These Endearing Young Charms

*The words to this Irish air were composed by Thomas Moore (1779-1852), who wrote new lyrics
to traditional tunes and performed them in the drawing rooms of the upper class.
It's also known as "My Lodging's in the Cold, Cold Ground."*

Traditional Irish
Arranged by Glenn Weiser

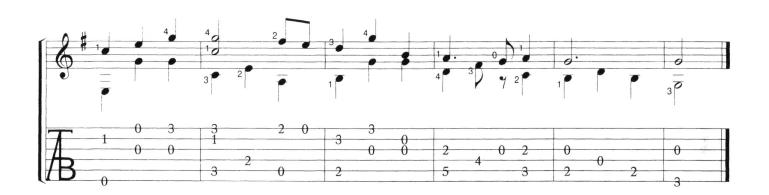

The Battle of Aughrim

*On July 11, 1691, the forces of William of Orange decisively defeated the Irish under
General Patrick Sarsfield at Aughrim Pass. This led to the siege of Limerick,
and Ireland's subsequent capitulation and sufferings at the hands of the English.*

Traditional Irish
Arranged by Glenn Weiser

16

The Boys of Wexford

This is a sprightly Irish march. It makes a good medley with "The Banks of Inverness."

Traditional Irish
Arranged by Glenn Weiser

Castles in the Air

This fancifully titled tune is a schottische, which is a 19th century round dance similar to a slow polka.

Traditional
Arranged by Glenn Weiser

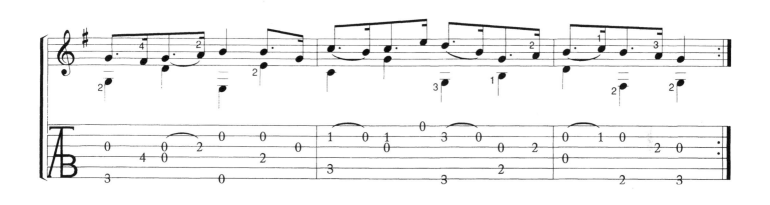

Childgrove

This is a haunting English country dance tune. It's also the only arrangement in the key of Dm in this book .

Traditional English
Arranged by Glenn Weiser

Cock Up Your Beaver

In this stately Scottish Jacobite song, a young man is encouraged to tilt his beaverskin hat at a rakish angle as he rides off to fight the English. Turlough O'Carolan wrote variations to the tune.

Traditional Scottish
Arranged by Glenn Weiser

Come Under My Plaidie

This Scottish song has a man of a certain age wooing a young lassie by promising her a comfortable married life. He tells her he can provide for her much better than the young man she really loves instead. Practicality prevails over romance, and she marries the older man. In Scots dialect, a plaidie is a plaid blanket.

Traditional Scottish
Arranged by Glenn Weiser

Dainty Davie

*This song tells the true story of a young man in Scotland who escaped
an English press gang by jumping through a window of a house into a maiden's bedroom.
He was most amorously received by the girl, and ended up marrying her.*

Traditional Scottish
Arranged by Glenn Weiser

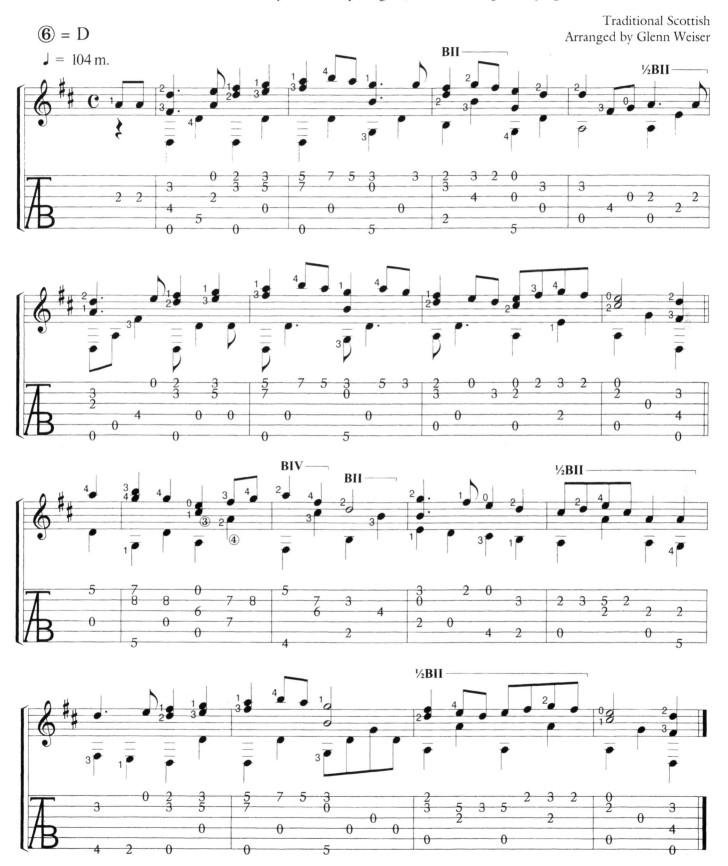

Down by the Sally Gardens

*This Irish love song had lyrics written to the melody by W.B. Yeats, who heard it sung
by an old man and could not remember the original words. Sally is used to make wicker furniture.*

Traditional Irish
Arranged by Glenn Weiser

24

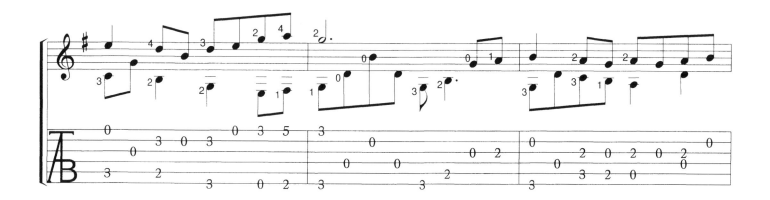

The Earl of Dalhousie's Happy Return

I learned this beautiful Scottish march from the playing of Cape Breton fiddler Natalie MacMaster.

Traditional Scottish
Arranged by Glenn Weiser

Eileen Aroon

This is a very famous and also very old Irish love song. It is ascribed to a 14th century harper named Carol O'Daly. When this tune was played for George Frederick Handel in 1742, he said that he would rather have been the composer of it than all his operas and oratorios. The two settings here are from "O'Neill's Music of Ireland," which is one the principal collections of traditional Irish Music.

First Setting

Carol O'Daly
Arranged by Glenn Weiser

⑥ = D

♩ = 84 m.

SECOND SETTING

Carol O'Daly
Arranged by Glenn Weiser

FLOW GENTLY, SWEET AFTON

Like Thomas Moore, the beloved Scottish poet Robert Burns (1759-1796) also wrote new lyrics
to traditional melodies. It was Burns who took down "Auld Lang Syne" from the singing of an old man.

Traditional Scottish
Arranged by Glenn Weiser

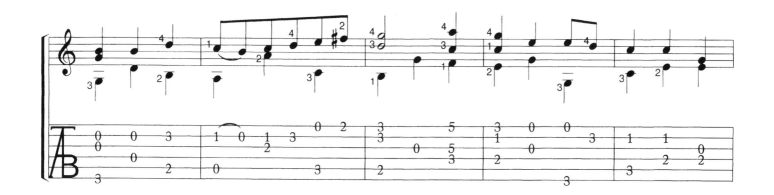

For Ireland I'd Not Tell Her Name

I learned this lovely air from Greg Schaaf, a tradtional musician from upstate New York.

Traditional Irish
Arranged by Glenn Weiser

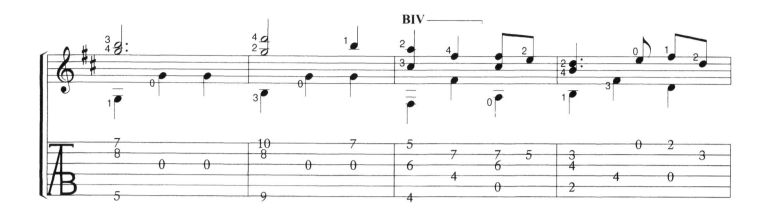

Hugh O'Neill's Lament

I found this slow Air in "O'Neills' Music of Ireland." Hugh O'Neill (d. 1616) was an Earl of Tyrone who renounced his title to take up his hereditary position as an Irish chieftain and fight the English. He led the Irish to victory in the Battle of The Yellow Ford in 1598, but was eventually subdued, after which he chose exile in France. Laments were often composed by traditional musicians at the passing of famous people.

Traditional Irish
Arranged by Glenn Weiser

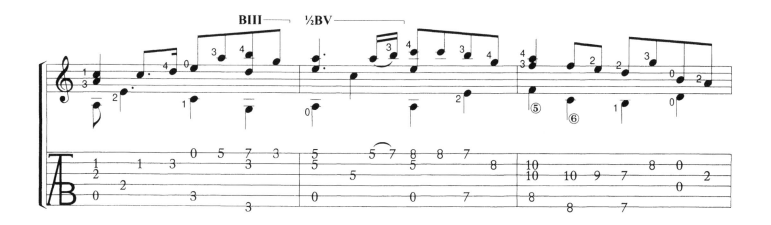

King of the Fairies

The poet W. B. Yeats once asked an old Irishwoman, "Do you believe in the fairies?"
"No," she replied, "but they're there."
Fingerstylist Eric Schoenberg can be heard playing this haunting air on his Rounder album "Steel Strings."

Traditional Irish
Arranged by Glenn Weiser

The Lark in the Clear Air

This serene tune is from "An Irish Tunebook."

Traditional Irish
Arranged by Glenn Weiser

38

The Lass of Patie's Mill

This a Scottish tune that was also played in Ireland. Carolan reworked it as "Carolan's Cap."

Traditional Scottish
Arranged by Glenn Weiser

Londonderry Air

This gorgeous air from Co. Derry is considered by musicologists one of the most perfectly conceived of all folk melodies. It's also been the victim of many maudlin renditions by Irish tenors. Stripped of the schmaltz, the melody shines in its original beauty.

Traditional Irish
Arranged by Glenn Weiser

MacPherson's Lament

This is the famous swan song of the Scotsman James MacPherson (1675–1700), who was a gifted fiddler and one of the founders of the strathspey style. Unfortunately, MacPherson was also a robber, for which he was eventually apprehended and sentenced to be hanged on the town of Banff. On the day of his execution the town fathers learned that a royal reprieve was on the way and pushed the town clock forward by one hour to seal his fate. MacPherson was led to the gallows, and played this beautiful tune, composed the night before. As a final gesture of defiance he then broke his fiddle over his knee and tossed it to the crowd, whereupon he was hanged.

Traditional Scottish
Arranged by Glenn Weiser

42

Neil Gow's Lament for his Second Wife

*Neil Gow (1727-1807) was the court fiddler to the Duke of Atholl in Scotland,
and a composer of traditional tunes. He was one of the masters of the strathspey style of fiddling,
which is characterized by a tendency to begin phrases with accented upbows.
Today you can see his violin and oil portrait at Blair Castle in Perthshire, the Duke's traditional residence.*

Neil Gow
Arranged by Glenn Weiser

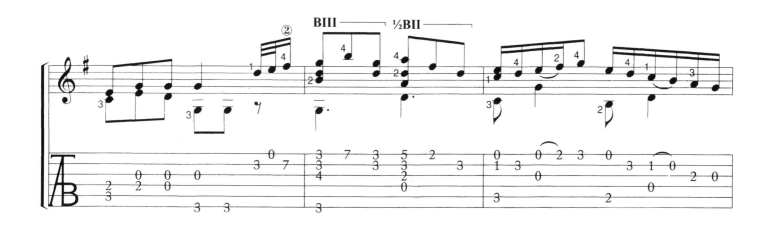

* Alternative Harmony, B part, measure 8

The Old Resting Chair

This slow air, written by the late Shetland fiddler Tom Anderson, suggests a mood of reverie.
I first heard it played by upstate New York fiddler George Wilson.

Tom Anderson
Arranged by Glenn Weiser

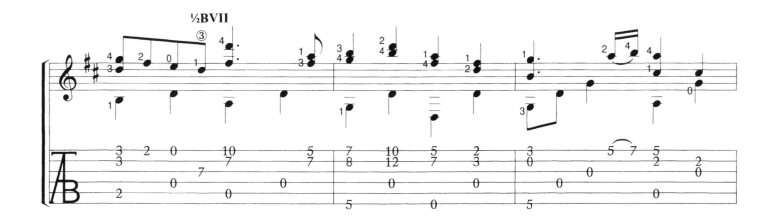

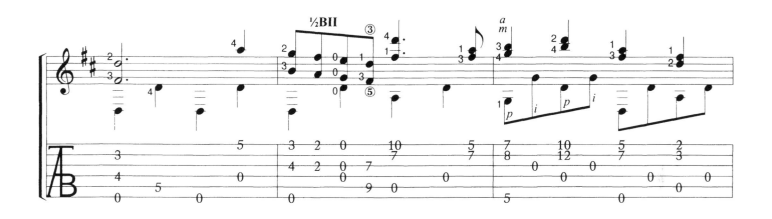

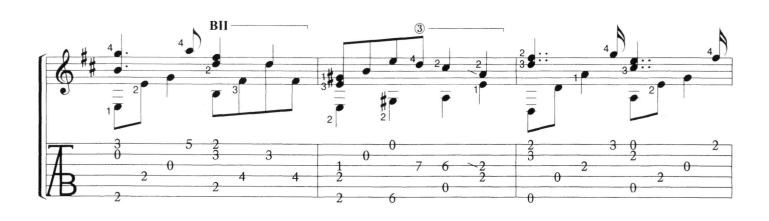

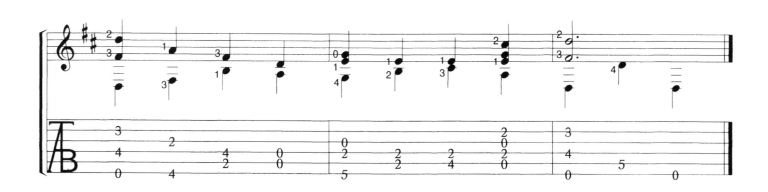

The Parting Glass

This mournful slow air can be found in a number of collections, the version here being close to the one found in "An Irish Tunebook, Vol. 1." The title suggests a final drink before the separation of friends.

Traditional Irish
Arranged by Glenn Weiser

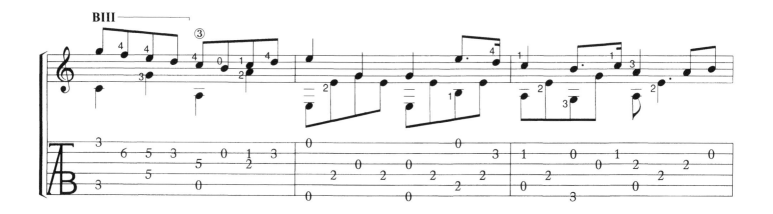

* Alternate Harmony, B part, measure 2

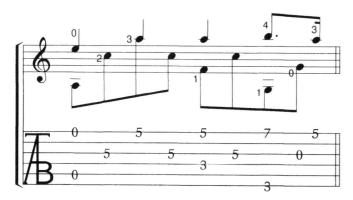

The Piper Through the Meadow Straying

Harper Derek Bell can be heard playing this air on "Derek Bell's Musical Ireland."
After I arranged it, I realized it was actually a variant of the Welsh Christmas carol "Deck the Halls."

Traditional Irish
Arranged by Glenn Weiser

Old Ireland, A Long Farewell

I found this plaintive air in "The Darley and McCall Collection of Traditional Irish Music."
There is an old Irish toast that runs "Long life to you, a child every year, and death in Ireland."
Emigration was a bitter pill to the Irish, and this tune captures the feeling that many must have felt
as they stood on the deck of a ship and saw the shore receding in the distance.

Traditional Irish
Arranged by Glenn Weiser

Princess Augusta

This is one of Neil Gow's compositions.

Neil Gow
Arranged by Glenn Weiser

The Rocks of the Brae

I learned this mournful Scottish air from Paul Rosenberg,
a traditional musician and dance caller in the Albany, NY, area.

Traditional Scottish
Arranged by Glenn Weiser

Scottish Farewell

*I learned this impassioned air from Robin Williamson's pennywhistle book but knew
nothing about it for years. Finally I met Scottish singer Norman Kennedy, who told me that it is a
Gaelic emigration song of the Highlands in which a young man bids a final farewell to his sweetheart.*

Traditional Scottish
Arranged by Glenn Weiser

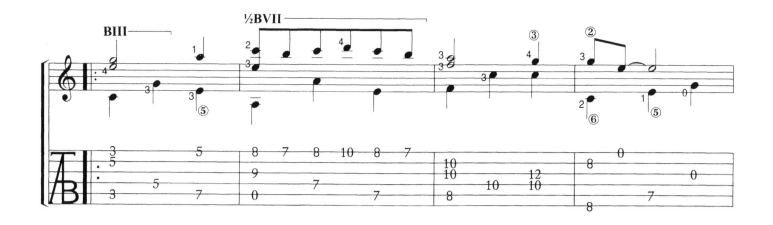

The Shepherd's Wife

This waltz comes from the hammer dulcimer playing of Bill Spence, who performs with Fenning's All Stars.

Traditional
Arranged by Glenn Weiser

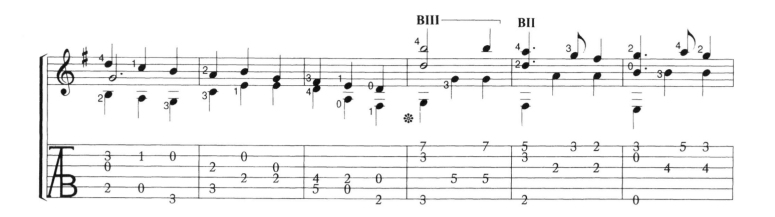

*Alternate Harmony, B part, measures 1 & 9

The Rose Tree

This tune is fairly old, as evidenced by the fact that it can be found in many variants.

Traditional
Arranged by Glenn Weiser

60

Hornpipes,
Jigs, and Reels

Alexander's Hornpipe

This setting is my own blending of two different versions.
There are differing opinions as to the validity of such composites; I say the end justifies the means.

Traditional Irish
Arranged by Glenn Weiser

The Brown Coffin

I found this one in "Irish Fiddle Tunes," published by Fiddlecase Books.
It reminds me of "The Battle Hymn of the Republic."

Traditional Irish
Arranged by Glenn Weiser

CLARK'S HORNPIPE

This is also known as "The Huntsman's Hornpipe" (a huntsman is the leader of a fox chase). It is also the only arrangement in this book in the key of D that is in standard tuning rather than the usual dropped D. Most hornpipes should be played with a dotted feel, but this should be played like a slow reel instead.

Traditional Irish
Arranged by Glenn Weiser

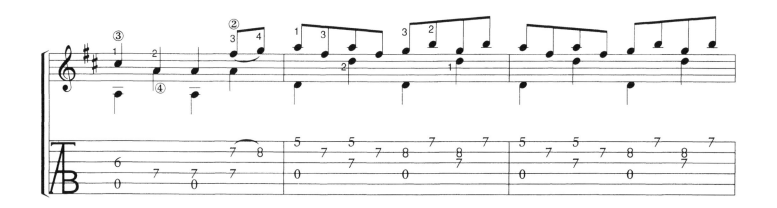

Delahanty's Hornpipe

This Irish hornpipe uses both the C sharp and C natural notes, and thus shares the qualities of two modes—in this case the major and the Mixolydian. Tunes like this are said to be "inflected."

Traditional Irish
Arranged by Glenn Weiser

The Fairies' Hornpipe

This can be heard on "The Chieftains 8." It's also in "O'Neill's."

Traditional Irish
Arranged by Glenn Weiser

Molly Halfpenny

After the harp died out in Ireland around 1800, her tunes were kept alive by fiddlers,
tinwhistle players, and pipers. This unusual hornpipe, which I learned from the tinwhistle playing of
Mary Bergin, is a descendant of the harp tune "Molly MacAlpin," by William Connellan (see my book
"Celtic Harp Music of Carolan and Others for Solo Guitar" for an arrangement of the original air).
Notice how the title got corrupted over the passage of time.

Traditional Irish
Arranged by Glenn Weiser

♩ = 126 m.

72

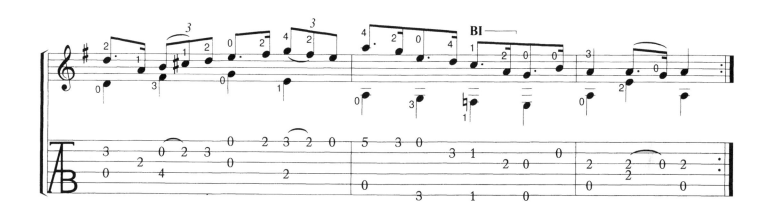

The Morpeth Rant

*Morpeth is a town in the northeast of England. A rant is a type of dance;
the tune is played like a fast hornpipe.*

Traditional Northumbrian
Arranged by Glenn Weiser

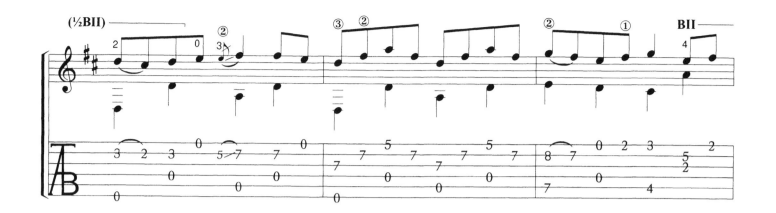

The Quindaro Hornpipe

I think this is originally a Scottish tune. Quindaro was a short-lived town (it was only inhabited for five years) on the banks of the Mississippi that was named after an Indian Queen.

Traditional Scottish
Arranged by Glenn Weiser

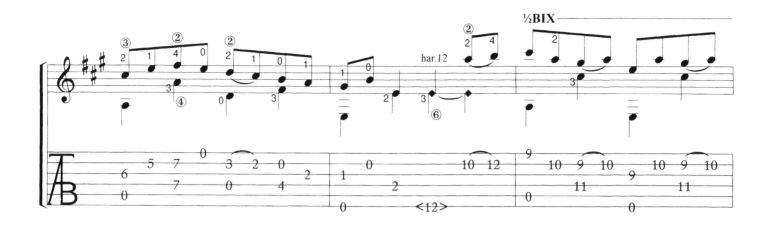

The Burnt Old Man

This Irish tune is a variant of the Scottish jig "The Campells are Coming."

Traditional Irish
Arranged by Glenn Weiser

Cherish the Ladies

Lovely title—and there's also a wonderful all-female Irish group of the same name.

Traditional Irish
Arranged by Glenn Weiser

The Connaughtman's Rambles

This well known tune has the gently rolling feel and carefree spirit found in many jigs.

Traditional Irish
Arranged by Glenn Weiser

Father Tom's Wager

This is a rollicking jig that covers a wide melodic range.
The arrangement is a little more advanced than some of the others.

Traditional Irish
Arranged by Glenn Weiser

The Joy of My Life

I learned this Irish tune from "O'Neill's."

Traditional Irish
Arranged by Glenn Weiser

82

The Lark in the Morning

This popular Irish tune has four parts.

Traditional Irish
Arranged by Glenn Weiser

84

85

Larry O' Gaff

This tune was played here in colonial times. It has been transposed up from G.

Traditional Irish
Arranged by Glenn Weiser

86

The Muckin' o' Geordie's Byre

This is a Scottish tune whose title roughly means "Slogging through George's barn."

Traditional Scottish
Arranged by Glenn Weiser

The Mooncoin Jig

This is something of a rarity—a Mixolydian jig in A.
There is also "The Mooncoin Reel," which, like the jig, can be found in "O'Neill's."

Traditional Irish
Arranged by Glenn Weiser

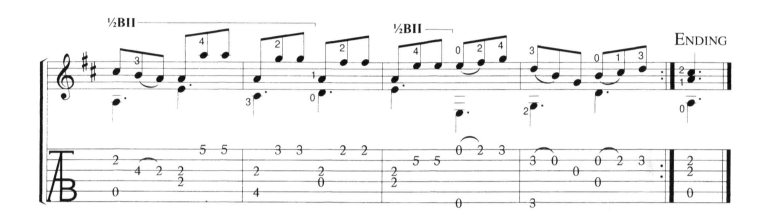

Nell Flaherty's Drake

This is a lively jig from "O'Neill's."
Note the three different harmonizations for each appearance of the opening theme.

Traditional Irish
Arranged by Glenn Weiser

O' Keefe's Slide

A slide is a type of jig from County Kerry in which the main accent occurs on the first beat
of every other measure (slides should really be written in 12/8 time, but they're not).
The tune is named after a famous Kerry fiddler who died around 1950.

Traditional Irish
Arranged by Glenn Weiser

Pipe on the Hob

A hob is a small ledge which projects from the side of a hearth on which things can be placed.
This A Dorian tune has three parts.

Traditional Irish
Arranged by Glenn Weiser

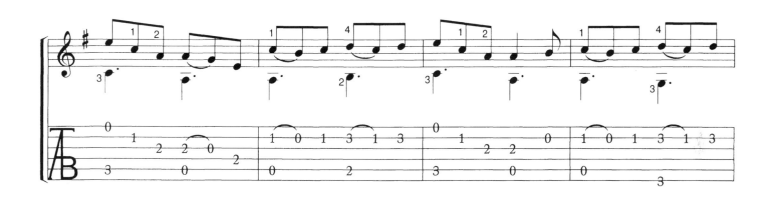

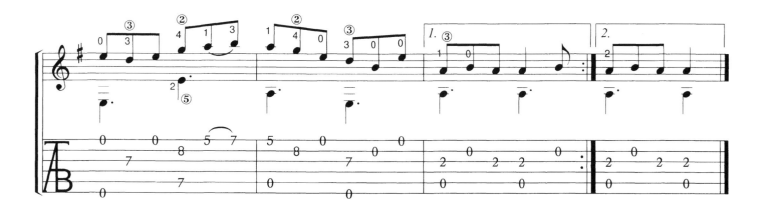

The Rakes of Kildare

A rake is a young "hot-shot" as well as a garden tool. This tune describes the former.
These kinds of titles—the boys or girls of such-and-such place—are common in Irish Music.

Traditional Irish
Arranged by Glenn Weiser

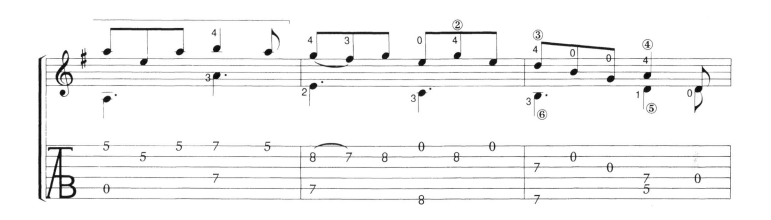

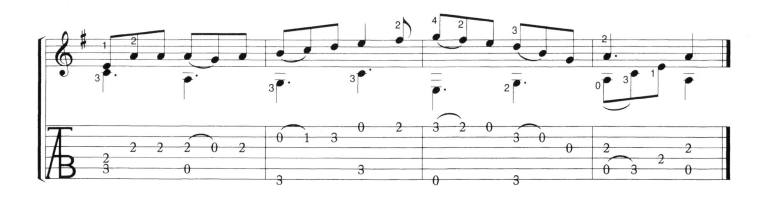

The Rock and the Wee Pickle Tow

The title of this sweet Scottish jig refers to articles used in spinning wool.
This tune comes from the playing of fiddler Alasdair Fraser. The original key is Bb.

Traditional Scottish
Arranged by Glenn Weiser

The Swallowtail Jig

This is a haunting E Dorian tune. By the way, there is also "The Swallowtail Reel."

Traditional Irish
Arranged by Glenn Weiser

The Trip to Sligo

Sligo is a center of traditional music in Ireland, and has its own fiddling style.
This in the Aeolian mode, or natural minor.

Traditional Irish
Arranged by Glenn Weiser

98

The Fairies' Reel

This was written in 1802 by Scottish fiddler Neil Gow for the Fife Hunt Ball.
It was carried to Appalachia by the settlers, where it became known as "Old Molly Hare."

Neil Gow
Arranged by Glenn Weiser

Angus Campell

*I learned this Scottish tune from the K-Tel record "25 Old Tyme Fiddle Hits," an anthology of
old chestnuts and an underground classic of traditional music. Unfortunately, none of the fiddlers are
credited on the record. In the 1st, 2nd, 5th & 6th measures of the B part, the pinky must barre over the first
two strings to play the notes A and E.*

Traditional Scottish
Arranged by Glenn Weiser

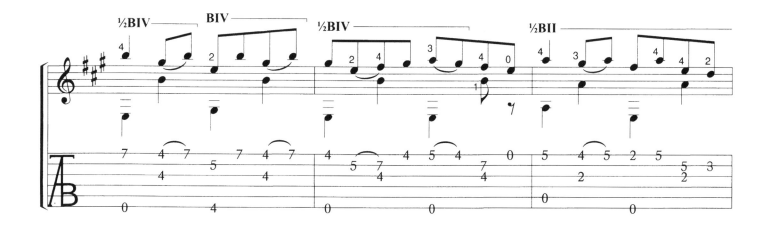

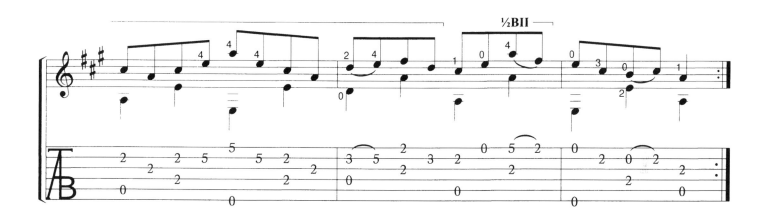

Cooley's Reel

This is one of the great E Dorian Irish reels. The triplet in the first measure has been simplified for the guitar, but if you want to attempt it anyway, it's been written out as a footnote.

Traditional Irish
Arranged by Glenn Weiser

* Advanced Variations, B part, measures 1, 2 & 5

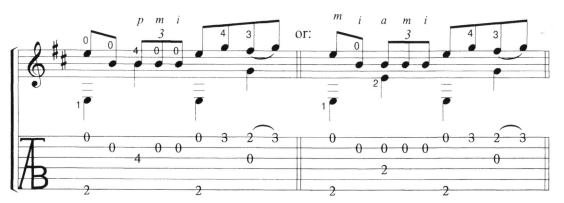

The Good-Natured Man

I learned this exuberant tune from "O'Neill's Music of Ireland."

Traditional Irish
Arranged by Glenn Weiser

Lord Gordon's Reel

This is a popular Scottish reel. Notice how it doesn't resolve at the end.

Traditional Scottish
Arranged by Glenn Weiser

Miss Monahan's Reel

This is a classic Irish reel in D.

Traditional Irish
Arranged by Glenn Weiser

The Mullingar Races

Mullingar is a town in Co. Westmeath famous for its greyhound races.

Traditional Irish
Arranged by Glenn Weiser

Peter Street

This Scottish reel is also known as "Timor the Tartar." The original key is A.

Traditional Scottish
Arranged by Glenn Weiser

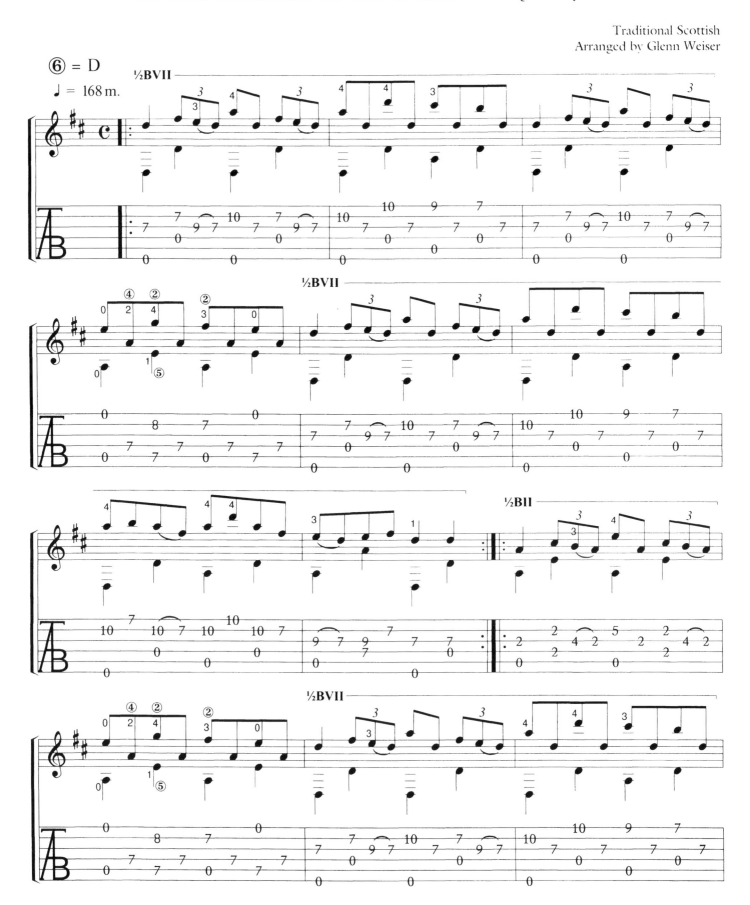

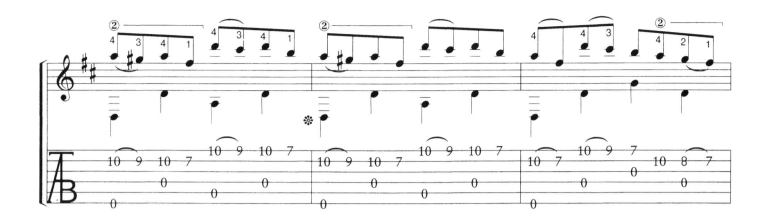

* Alternate Harmony, B part, measure 6

Petronella

This a Scottish reel, to which there is a New England contradance.
Petronella, by the way, was the daughter of St. Peter.

PIGEON ON THE GATE

This E Dorian tune is one of my favorite Irish reels.
In the first part, it seems, the pigeon lands on the gate; in the second, it takes flight.
In the footnote there is a more advanced version of the first measure containing a triplet.

Traditional Irish
Arranged by Glenn Weiser

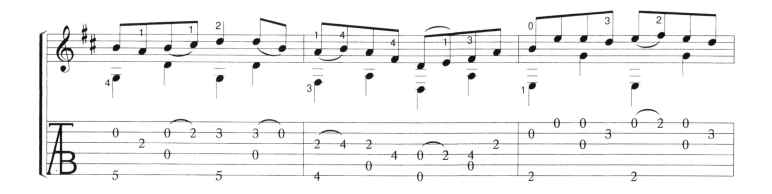

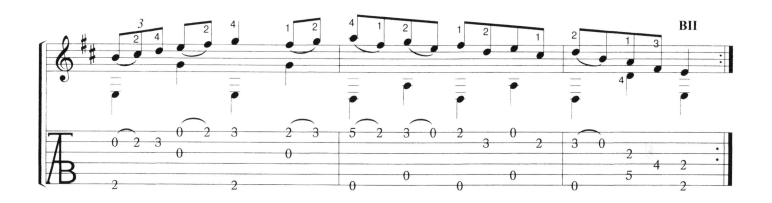

* Advanced Variation

The Pigtown Fling

*Old timey players know this Irish tune as "Stoney Point." The Irish version has two parts;
the American three. I've taken the liberty of including the third part in this setting.*

Traditional Irish
Arranged by Glenn Weiser

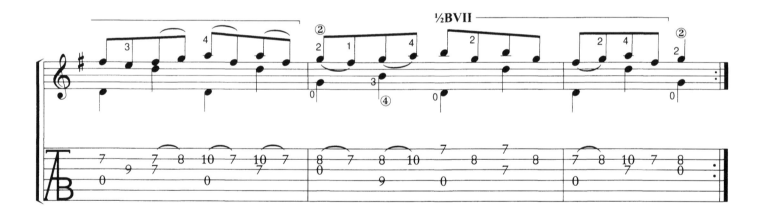

Scollay's Reel

This reel is from the Shetland Islands and was collected by folklorist Patrick Shuldham-Shaw.
It is a variant of the Irish tune "King of the Fairies," an arrangement of which
can be found on page 36. The original key is E minor.

Traditional Shetland
Arranged by Glenn Weiser

The Silver Spire

This Irish reel is said to be an elaboration of the Highland pipe march "Scotland the Brave."
It's also known in New England as "The Great Eastern," which was the first steamship to cross the Atlantic.

Traditional Irish
Arranged by Glenn Weiser

* Alternate Fingering, A part, measure 4

The Star of Munster

If the song "Star of the County Down" is any indicator,
the title of this A Dorian reel refers to an Irish beauty.

Traditional Irish
Arranged by Glenn Weiser

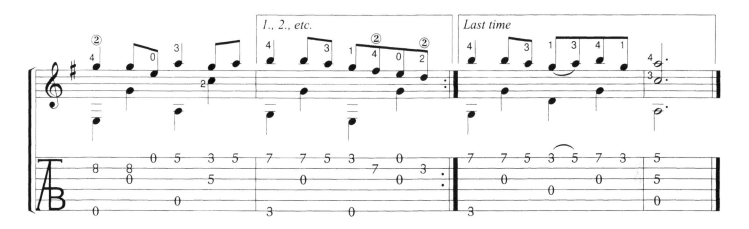

* Alternate Harmony, B part, measures 2, 3 & 4

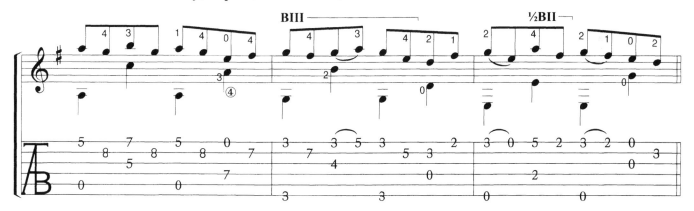

The Wise Maid

I learned this serpentine tune from Linda Baker, a traditional musician in the Albany, NY, area.
Note the arpeggios in the second part.

Traditional Irish
Arranged by Glenn Weiser

126

* Alternate Fingering, B part, measure 6

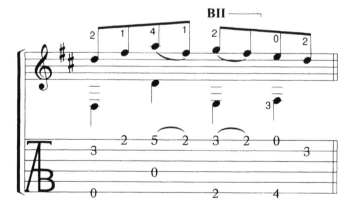

127

The Wind that Shakes the Barley

This Irish tune is a single reel, which is characterized by a four measure repeating A part and an eight measure non-repeating B part.

Traditional Irish
Arranged by Glenn Weiser

TUNES FROM "THE BUNTING COLLECTION"

The Dawning of the Day

This lovely harp tune has a hymnlike quality to it. It was collected from William Carr,
who at age 15 was the youngest performer at the Belfast festival. This air was arranged as a personal
memorial to a close friend, the late Athena Kouzan. What is death but the dawning of a new day?

Traditional Irish
Arranged by Glenn Weiser

131

The Foggy Dew

The major key version of this air was collected by Bunting from one J. MacKnight of Belfast in 1839. Even though the minor key setting is not in the Bunting collection, I have included it here anyway for the sake of comparison. The lyrics to this second version describe the Easter uprising of 1916, and can be heard on the Cheiftans album "The Long Black Veil" sung by Sinead O' Connor.

Major Key Version

Traditional Irish
Arranged by Glenn Weiser

Minor Key Version

Traditional Irish
Arranged by Glenn Weiser

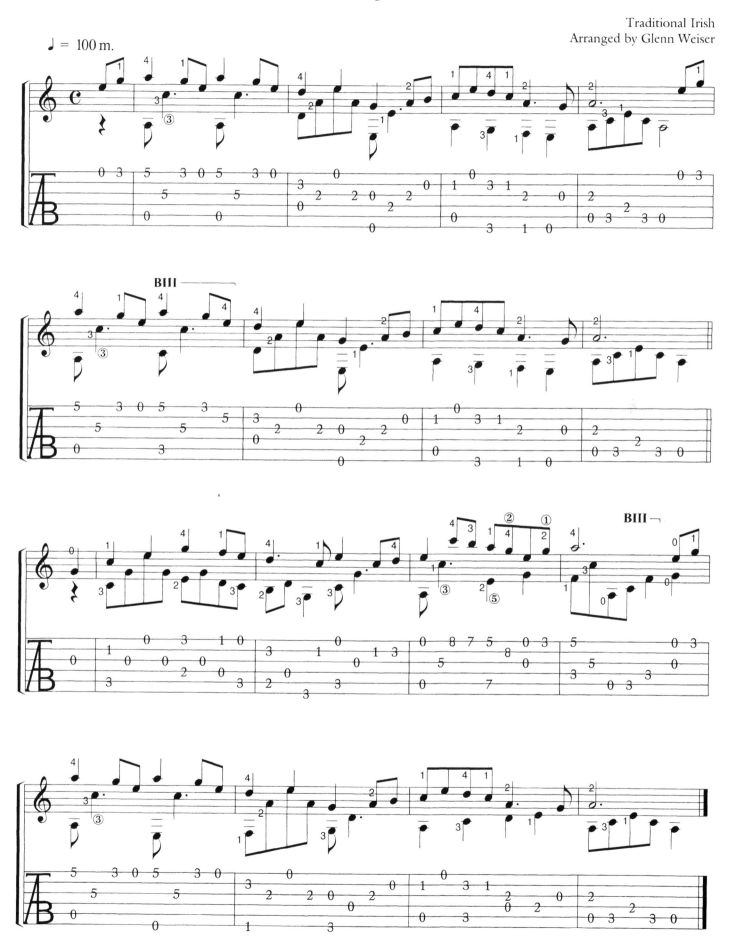

The Gentle Maiden

Now a popular waltz, this was taken down from the singing of a Miss Murphy in Dublin in 1839.

Traditional Irish
Arranged by Glenn Weiser

134

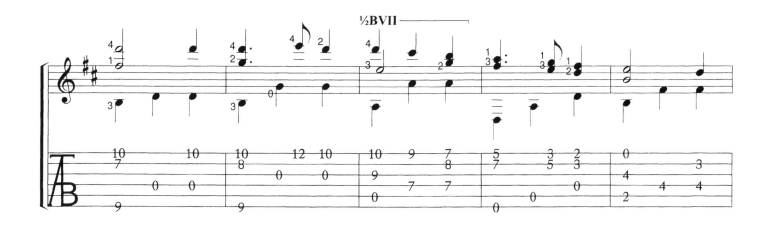

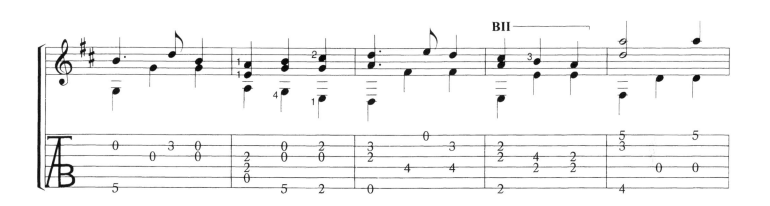

The Girl I Left Behind Me

This tune is probably Irish and is usually thought of as a fife march.
Bunting collected it from the harper Arthur O'Neill in 1800.

Traditional Irish
Arranged by Glenn Weiser

136

Give Me Your Hand

There is a famous story about this lovely tune, composed by Irish harper Rory O'Cahan.
While in Scotland, he once visited the castle of a Lady Eglington, who, taking him for a commoner, called for
a tune in a curt manner. O'Cahan took offense at this and left the the place in anger. When Lady Eglington
learned of his status she arranged a reconciliation and O'Cahan returned with this tune as a peace offering.
"Give Me Your Hand" soon became famous all over Scotland, and O'Cahan was eventaully summoned
for a command performance to the court of James VI of Scotand, who later as James I succeeded Elizabeth I
to the English throne. After the played the tune, the monarch was so inspired that that he arose,
walked over to O'Cahan and laid his hand on the harper's shoulder in a gesture of approval.
"A greater hand than thine has laid upon my shoulder," O'Cahan said.
"Who is that, man?" cried the King.
"The O'Neill, my leige," said the bold O'Cahan, referring the chieftain of Ulster.

Rory O'Cahan
Arranged by Glenn Weiser

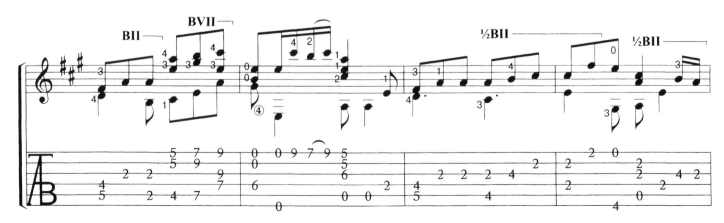

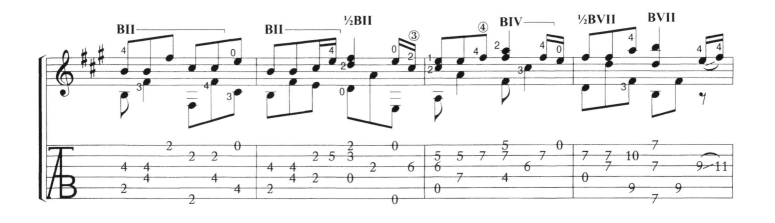

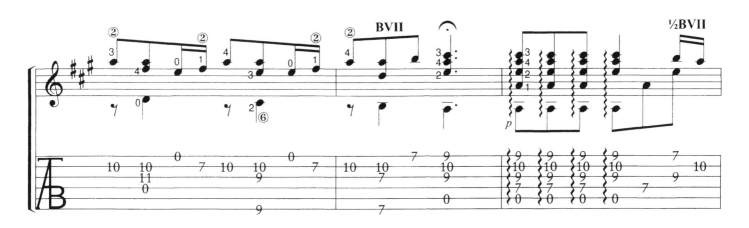

The Joyce's Country Greeting

Also known by its Gaelic name "An Speic Seoigheach," this is a harp tune in the ancient style. I have never encountered a melody quite like it. You can hear it on "The Best of The Chieftains." The Joyce's Country lies near the west coast of Ireland, in a region that has some of the most spectacular scenery in the Emerald Isle.

Traditional Irish
Arranged by Glenn Weiser

Saint Patrick's Day

Also known as "St. Patrick's Day in the Morning," most versions of this jig have an incomplete B part of six measures. I found a variant in the "Roche Collection" with the missing two measures and have included them here. Fiddler Frankie Gavin does a bangup job on this tune on his solo recording "Frankie Goes to Town."

Traditional Irish
Arranged by Glenn Weiser

A Soft Mild Morning

This gentle harp tune was taken down from the playing of Denis Hempson in 1796.

Irish Harp Air
Arranged by Glenn Weiser

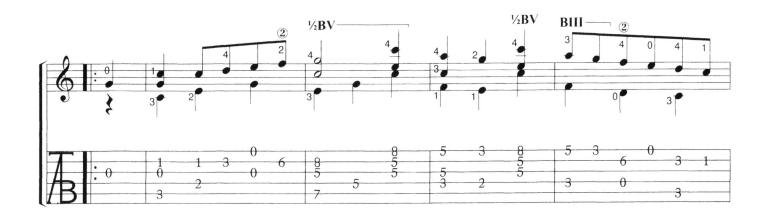

* Alternate Version, A Part, measure 9

Summer is Coming

This is a version of the English round "Summer is Icumen In," which dates from around 1250 and is the oldest decipherable piece of music in existence. At the beginning of summer the Irish would gather and sing this to welcome in the season. This is the only Celtic tune I have arranged in F. Incidentally, the repeats at the end are mine.

Traditional Irish
Arranged by Glenn Weiser

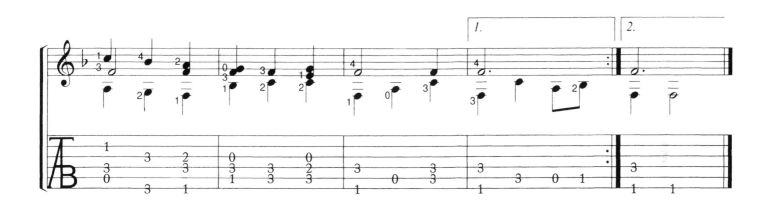

The Wild Geese

After the fall of Limerick in 1691, many who fought with the Irish Army chose exile in France or Spain rather than life under English rule. On the occasion of one departure, it is believed that a crowd of women gathered on the shore and sang this song as the ship with their men aboard sailed off. This is one the most poignant of all Irish airs, and Bunting himself held it in high esteem. It was noted from the harper Patrick Quinn in 1803.

Traditional Irish
Arranged by Glenn Weiser

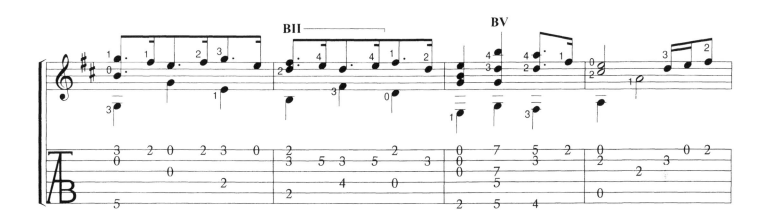

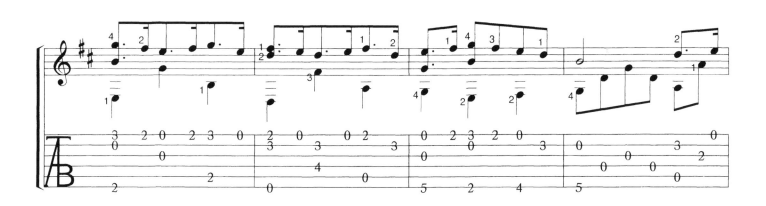

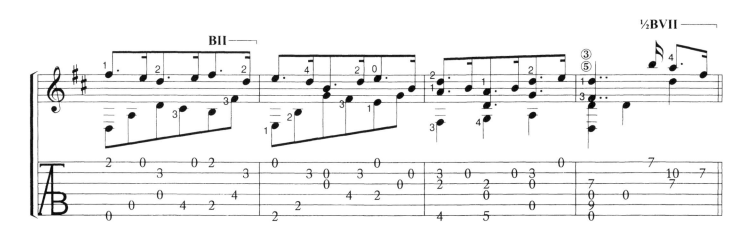

150

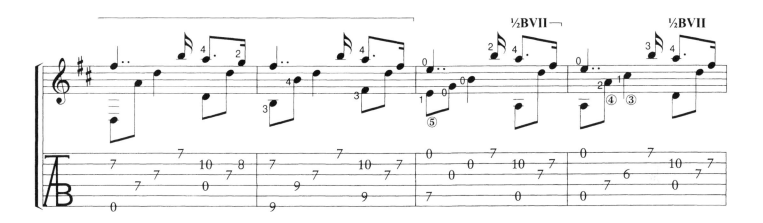

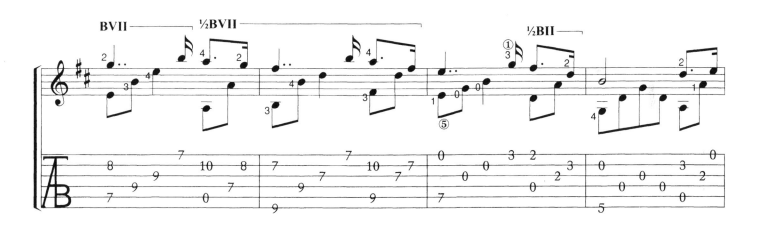

The Coolin

This very old tune was taken down from the playing of Denis Hempson, who was then over 100 years old and the last harper to play in the traditional manner of plucking the strings with long, crooked nails. The coolin was a thirteenth century men's hair style in which the back was grown long and the front was cropped. The English government became so consternated when young English men began to adopt the new look that they passed a law in 1295 forbidding it. In this beautiful song, an Irish maiden is exhorting other young women to marry the wearers of the coolin.

Traditional Irish
Arranged by Glenn Weiser

Harp Tunes of Turlough O'Carolan

Thomas Burke

This arrangement is based on Derek Bell's version of the tune, which is different than O'Sullivan's.
The Honorable Thomas Burke was a son of the 9th Earl of Clanricard.
Carolan wrote airs for several members of the family.

Carolan
Arranged by Glenn Weiser

Madam Cole

The 19th century Irish tune collector George Petrie calls this "one of Carolan's finest airs,"
and O'Sullivan agrees. It is considered to be more in the Italian style than the Irish.

Carolan
Arranged by Glenn Weiser

157

John Drury (First Air)

Carolan composed this for the wedding of John Drury and Elizabeth Goldsmith in 1724. Because the groom's family was wealthy and the bride's was not, Carolan praises those who marry for love rather than money in the lyrics. Incidentally, the bride was a cousin of Oliver Goldsmith, who wrote "The Vicar of Wakefield".

Carolan
Arranged by Glenn Weiser

⑥ = D

♩. = 100 m.

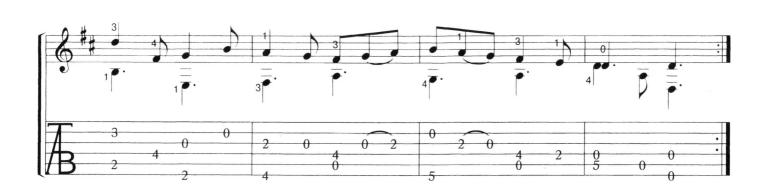

Anne MacDermott Roe

The MacDermott Roe family of Aldersford, Co. Roscommon, were Carolan's principal
patrons and oldest friends. Carolan was given his schooling and harp lessons by them,
and it was to their home that he returned when he knew that his time was not long.

Carolan
Arranged by Glenn Weiser

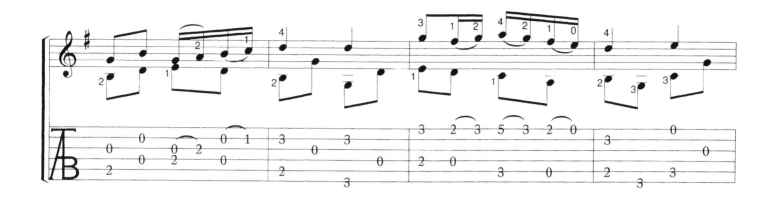

Miss MacDermott

This is thought to have been written for a daughter of the MacDermott Roes of Coolavin, who were related to Carolan's patrons of the same name at Aldersford. The Coolavin branch were descended from from royalty, which is why the tune is also known as "The Princess Royal." A later variant of this tune can be found in "O'Neill's" as the set dance "Rodney's Glory," the title of which celebrates a famous English naval victory.

Carolan
Arranged by Glenn Weiser

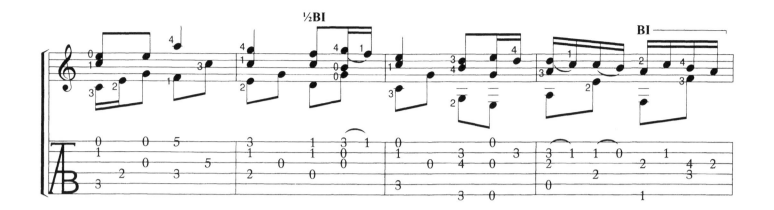

Denis O'Conor (Second Air)

Like the MacDermott Roes, the O'Conors of Belangore were among Carolan's most devoted patrons.
Denis, the head of the family, was descended from an Irish king.

Carolan
Arranged by Glenn Weiser

Maurice O'Connor (Second Air)

Maurice O'Connor was a Catholic who had to convert to Protestantism in order to practice law in England, where he became wealthy. This is a very pretty tune.

Carolan
Arranged by Glenn Weiser

John Kelly

The subject of this graceful air is uncertain.

Carolan
Arranged by Glenn Weiser

Mary O'Neill

This is one of the few tunes Coralan wrote in the Mixolydian mode. O'Sullivan credits Francis O'Neill, compiler of "O'Neill's Music of Ireland," with having found the correct title.

Carolan
Arranged by Glenn Weiser

ENDING

John O'Reilly

This is the longest extant version of the tune, all others having two parts only.
The other parts may have been added later by a piper or fiddler.

Carolan
Arranged by Glenn Weiser

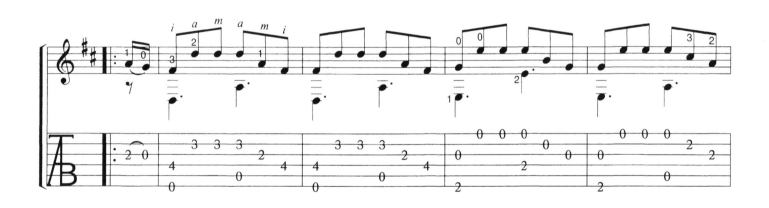
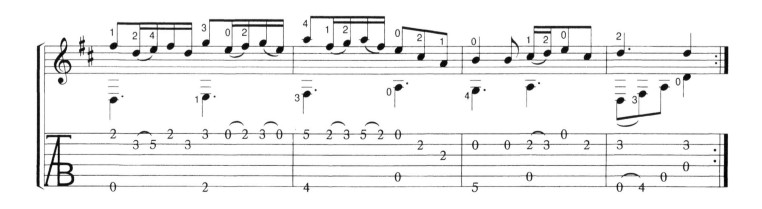

*Alternate Fingering, B part, measure 10

Kean O'Hara (Third Air)

Carolan's authorship of this tune is uncertain, but it is very sweet nonetheless.

Carolan
Arranged by Glenn Weiser

Planxty Scott

This slow jig is from "O'Neill's."
Donal O'Sullivan dismissed the name as unverifiable and simply listed it as No. 179.

Carolan
Arranged by Glenn Weiser

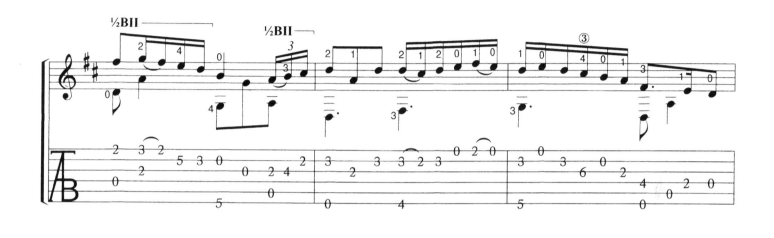

175

Captain Sudley

This tune, also known as "Carolan's Dowry," was composed for the wedding of Carolan's daughter Siobhan to a Protestant military officer. Even though Carolan, who was a devout Catholic, seems to have disapproved of the match, he composed the tune anyway and called it his "dowry."

Carolan
Arranged by Glenn Weiser

177

Colonel Palmer

This jig can be found on Derek Bell's second album.

Carolan
Arranged by Glenn Weiser

All Alive

This jig was ascribed to Carolan by George Petrie.

Carolan
Arranged by Glenn Weiser

Carolan's Cottage

This is from "O'Neill's Music of Ireland." O'Sullivan doesn't say much about it except to compare its structure to "The Lament for Terence MacDonough."

Carolan
Arranged by Glenn Weiser

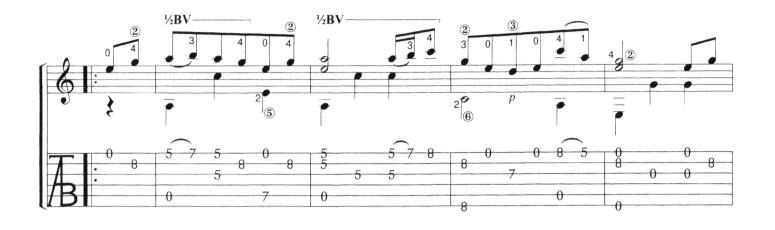

Carolan's Fancy

Originally published in 1810 in John Mulholland's "Collection of Ancient Irish Airs" under the title "Planxty Safaigh," this was renamed "Carolan's Fancy" by Derek Bell. O'Sullivan lists it as "No. 174."

Carolan
Arranged by Glenn Weiser

Planxty O'Carolan

This was published in "O'Neill's Music of Ireland." O'Sullivan doubted the veracity of the title and listed it as No. 177. In measure eight of the second part, the original version has a rest instead of the quarter note G, which I have substituted instead. I believe the original melody note was a G played by the bass hand and therefore not taken down.

Carolan
Arranged by Glenn Weiser

The Two William Davises

This is Carolan's reworking of the Scottish tune "Killiecrankie," which was probably written by the Irish harper Thomas Connelan shortly after the Battle of Killiecrankie on 27th July, 1689. Carolan's lyrics of the song contrast a miserly father and generous son of the same name.

Carolan
Arranged by Glenn Weiser

⑥ = D

♩ = 120 m.

The Lament for Terence MacDonough

Terence MacDonough of Sligo was a "distinguished and versatile Irishman," being a soldier, lawyer, man of affairs, poet, and patron of poets. This elegy, composed upon his death, was later arranged by Beethoven for the Scottish music publisher George Thompson ("Irish and Scottish Songs"—Opus 108).

Carolan
Arranged by Glenn Weiser

Ode to Whiskey

Carolan's authorship of this tune is uncertain. In translation, the lyrics begin
"Why, liquor of life, do I love you so, when in all our encounters you lay me low?"

Carolan
Arranged by Glenn Weiser

Alphabetical Index

Throughout the book, in each section, tunes are arranged roughly in alphabetical order, though some tunes have been moved to minimize page-turns. In the Carolan section, the tunes for Carolan's patrons are given first.

GLENN WEISER

Glenn Weiser was born in 1952 in Ridgewood, New Jersey and began playing guitar at thirteen. While in high school, he studied classical guitar with Paul Battat, who was a student of Andrés Segovia's pupil Rodrigo Rierez. Later, he studied steel string fingerpicking with ragtime guitarist Eric Schoenberg and also took up harmonica, banjo, and mandolin. Glenn is the author of several books for guitar and harmonica, his most recent being *Celtic Harp Music of Carolan and Others for Solo Guitar*. He has also written for the magazines *Acoustic Guitar*, *Sing Out!*, and *Acoustic Musician*. Glenn currently teaches guitar in the Albany, New York, area and performs in the Northeast.